Shepton Mallet

A Visible History

by Alan Stone

photographs by Tony Patten

foreword by Fred Davis MBE

Published in 2005 by
Shepton Mallet Local History Group
10 Society Road, Shepton Mallet, Somerset BA4 5GF

email sheptonhistory@btinternet.com

Printed by Creeds the Printers, Broadoak, Bridport. Dorset. DT6 5NL

ISBN 0-9548125-1-4

Foreword - By Fred Davies MBE

Shepton Mallet - A visible history

Whether you are a casual visitor to the town, mildly interested, or a serious student of local history, 'Shepton Mallet - A visible history' provides a perfect introduction to the rich tapestry of the town's local history.

For some 5,000 years settlers have been attracted to the Shepton Mallet area. Maesbury Hill Fort crowns the Mendip Ridge above the town, its double-ditched and embanked hill fort developed during the last millennium BC. A little to the east, on the crest of Beacon Hill is another reminder of that almost forgotten age with a scatter of round barrows.

The Romans establishing a settlement which stretched from Cannards Grave to Charlton on either side of the Fosse Way which ran in an almost straight line from Exeter to Lincoln, passing the east side of Shepton Mallet. As the Romans withdrew during the fifth century, so the settlement at Fosse Lane declined and was soon deserted but for perhaps one or two subsistence farms.

Now it was the time of the Saxons and the first written record of Shepton Mallet which is contained in a charter of Inna, King of the West Saxons dated AD 705 in which he gave all the lands on both sides of the river from Doulting to Correges Cumb (Croscombe), to the Abbots of Glastonbury. The Saxons founded a new settlement, not at Charlton, but a little further west, that formed the basis of Shepton Mallet today. The hand of the Saxon mason can still be seen in the chisel-marks on the dressed stone within our parish church.

The Norman invasion of 1066 brought in William the Conquerer's retinue a knight named William Malet and among his many grants was Shepton to which he appended his name, making Shepton Mallet among one of the earliest double place names.

It is said that a vigorous woollen industry was already well established in the Mendips during the 11th century and Shepton Mallet's growth and development was a direct result of the woollen industry. In 1394 Croscombe and Shepton Mallet were each producing between 200 and 800 broadcloths a year with local products finding their way to Bilbao and Sesbastion for example, in bundles of ten cloths; light popinjay greens, light sky colours and fine stamell reds among other shades. Clothiers rose to the rank of gentry and many fine houses in the town today is a legacy of those affluent days.

By the mid-nineteenth century the town saw the final demise of the monopoly of woollen industry, and then in came brewing; Oakhill Brewery (1767), then in the parish of Shepton, Charlton Brewery (1844), and The Anglo Bavarian Brewery (1864), the later having the proud boast of being the first lager brewery in the country.

Foreword (Cont)

All this, and much more has left its indelible stamp on the town - visible reminders of the colourful and sometimes turbulent past. Shepton Mallet - A visible history, doesn't claim to be a complete history of the town, for that would take many volumes, but it does provide a valuable introduction to the history of this ancient Market Town.

The use of modern-day photographs, combined with much earlier comparisons, brings much of our local heritage to life in an evocative, easy to follow, way and is a valuable resource for anyone mildly interested in, or a serious student of, local history.

Fred Davis MBE
April 2005.

Acknowledgements

The majority of the photographs for this publication come from a vast selection taken around Shepton Mallet by Tony Patten during 2004 and early 2005. Tony, recently retired from a career glodetrotting for the United Nations, is Secretary of the Shepton Mallet TIC and Heritage Centre.

Photographs from the Fred Davis Collection: Numbers 17a, 21, 29a, 38, 19b and advert, 41a, 41b, 42, 44, 44a, 50a, 50c.

Other photographs and images, old and new, have been provided by Alan Stone, Richard Stone, Kai Roth-Thomas, Janet Moore and Francis Disney BEM

Attempts have been made to trace owners of all images. I apologise should any have been inadvertantly missed.

Thanks

In addition to those already mentioned thanks must be offered to Lorraine Pratten, Manager of the Shepton Mallet TIC and Heritage Centre, and Christine Oram and David Williams of the Shepton Mallet Local History Group. Thanks must also be offered to Tony Patten and my wife Christine for attempting to correct the spelling in the proof - the remaining mistakes are mine!

Alan Stone, April 2005

Shepton Mallet - A visible history

Some find history a dry sort of subject, only accessible by looking in books and reading; irrelevant to modern life. However television documentaries with extensive re-enactments and explanation have now brought the subject alive for many people and there is a renewed wave of interest in our historic heritage.

Strangely, one of the most accessible aspects of history is still largely ignored, unless it is particularly attractive. The buildings in the streets around us tell us far more about our past than we would give them credit for. This short book has a simple purpose. To look at the buildings around Shepton Mallet and see what story they have to tell us about our rich historic heritage.

The book combines photographs of what can be seen today interspersed with older photographs to give some

1) Town Street from north

idea of historic context. Grouped by different themes it gives a 'by subject' as well as geographical introduction to some of the major aspects of the history of the town.

Numbering each of the photographs will allow them to be located on the map and for it to be used to plan walks, or just used for reference when out and about in the town. It is written for both residents and visitors who want to find out a little more about what they see. In no way does this claim to be a full history of Shepton Mallet, but hopefully it will

1a) Town Street from north 1859

introduce aspects of history, which over a period of time can be researched further. In the case of Shepton Mallet, the buildings we have now provide clues to a largely unwritten past.

This short work draws extensively on the limited published sources of Shepton Mallet History and these are identified for people who wish to study further.

The Market Square

The first mention of a market in Shepton Mallet was in 1232, which apparently Wells successfully objected to. However, in 1318 Edward II granted a market charter to Cicely de Beauchamp. It is probable that the Market Square was the site of this market from the start. As the town shows some signs of planning, being 'laid out' in a regular pattern, it is possible that the market square arises from this. However it has certainly been the location of the market since the later mediaeval period.

2) Market Cross, Market Place

Apparently the Market, as with most markets, was often the scene of rowdy or disreputable happenings. One legend is that the last wife auction in Britain was held here. The headmaster of the Grammar School, John Farbrother, writing in 1859, said: "Sales of so unnatural a character as knocking down your wife to the highest bidder, have on several occasions, been transacted here. At the last of these, which was accidentally witnessed by a lady, whose authority I cite, the 'better half' was coolly handed over for a crown, with a halter round her neck."

The Market Square is dominated by the Market Cross the shape of which, in these brand conscious days, has become a recognizable 'logo' for the town. The cross was built in 1500 as a memorial to Walter Buckland and his wife, and according to its listing schedule the unusual five-sided central core dates from this period. The hexagonal arrangement of arches around it, under which traders could set up their stalls is thought to date from 1700. Old illustrations show that the upper spire of the Market Cross has been changed a few times with extensive alterations in both the 18th and 19th centuries.

The Market Square has long been the historic hub of the town. It was here that there was a clash between the Royalists, with support from Wells, and the locally supported Parliamentarians during the English Civil War. The Duke of Monmouth passed through it during his attempt to seize the crown in 1685 and subsequently the notorious Judge Jeffreys sentenced 12 men to be hanged in the Market Square; their bodies to be hung from the Market Cross to discourage future attempts at rebellion.

Nearby is the ancient Shambles, a reminder of the two long rows of market stalls that once stretched across the market square and from which traders sold their wares. The name derives from the Saxon 'scammel' for butchers slab. The ancient monument listing has recently been removed from the Shambles as it is thought that none of its fabric is still original. However, this is harsh as they would have been patched and repaired throughout their long life

2a) The Shambles

and this rare survival is not an ornamental reconstruction, indeed it is occasionally used by charities on a Saturday morning for its original purpose, and during the Friday market the fruit and vegetable stall uses it to stack produce on.

However the Shambles have not always been considered an attractive aspect of the market place. In the 1850s the Shepton Mallet Journal was campaigning for their removal

2b) The Amulet (Centre)

believing the 'gallows like structures' were a blight on the appearance of the town.

The most controversial building in the Market Square is without doubt the 'Amulet' which was known as the 'Centre' when it was opened in 1975 as part of a major town centre redevelopment, gifted to the town by Francis Showering, the Babycham millionaire. Unfortunately the building has never managed to fulfill the aims of its benefactor. The building may have been too ambitious to fulfill its original purpose of putting some

2c) Market Place 1859

heart back into what was already seen as a failing town centre. A combination of problems with design, location, size and inconsistent management by the local authorities (to put it mildly) has turned what should at least have been a positive building for the town into something of a white elephant. At the time of writing its future is 'uncertain' a mixture of wild plans and a decaying building needing repairs. However this has been a similar story for the past twenty years.

Many locals for some reason now believe that the Amulet deprived the Market Square of a view of the church. Photographs prove that this was not the case. The building it replaced was a utilitarian late Victorian block which housed both the Urban and Rural district councils. This itself, replaced previous buildings on the site, which were again between the Market Square and the Church.

2d) Library (Bunch of Grapes)

The Library building on the north side of the square has every appearance of being the old Bunch of Grapes Public House. In fact it was rebuilt at the time of the 1970s town centre reconstruction, the original having been supposedly demolished without permission.

The buildings around the south and west would appear to date mainly from the nineteenth century but must be built on the remains of earlier buildings. The Bell Inn contains a bell on its front. This is reputed to be the bell which was rung to start trading at the weekly market. The pig market used to be in the yard to the rear of the Bell Hotel. Evidence in the county record office suggests this went back at least as early as the seventeenth century.

The part of the Market Place in front of the Bell Hotel and Lloyds Bank has on occasion been referred to as 'The Corn Pitching'. Mendip District Council referred to it as such when they were doing street 'enhancements' (Yorkshire 'setts') in 1993. A former town historian, the late Mabs Holland, believed the misunderstanding over the name came about from a turnpike notice she had reproduced for a Victorian Evening held in the town in 1990. The notice was issued in 1832 after the Shepton Mallet Turnpike had bought a building that used to stand in this area to demolish it to allow the Stagecoach from Bristol to run through the town. They were merely anxious to ensure that the market did not spread over the roadway they had so recently cleared.

SHEPTON-MALLET
TURNPIKE.

THE Commissioners of this Trust do hereby give Notice, that they will not permit or suffer any GOODS, WARES, or MERCHANDIZE, (save and except CORN, which is allowed to be pitched Toll Free,) to be placed or exposed for Sale upon the open space of ground in front of the BELL INN, in SHEPTON-MALLET, the property of this Trust; and any person or persons so placing or exposing the same for Sale, (save and except as aforesaid,) will be Prosecuted as the Law directs.

By order of the Trustees:

T. H. HELE PHIPPS,

Shepton-Mallet, 5th Sept., 1832.   CLERK.

CARY, PRINTER, SHEPTON-MALLET

2e) Corn Pitching?

2f) Market Square

9

The Church and around

The earliest evidence of Christianity in the West Country is the Chi-Rho Amulet found in an archeological dig off the Fosse Way (Roman road) in the eastern part of Shepton Mallet, and dated to the 3rd or 4th century AD. This site has now been revealed as the third most significant Roman town in Somerset, though with none of the grand buildings like those found in Bath. Shepton Mallet, according to many historians, then seems to have disappeared off the map in the 'dark ages' for a few centuries being merely lands belonging to the monks of Glastonbury Abbey. Recent archeological digs and the standing evidence of Saxon remains in the stone church of St Peter and St Paul seem to suggest this may not be the case.

3) The Chi-Rho Amulet

Is it possible that a religious community in Shepton Mallet was 'taken over' by Glastonbury Abbey which then assumed its mantle through the spin of its marketing men? There is a report by a William of Worcester that St Indractus and Drusa were buried in Shepton, though William of Malmesbury claims this honour for Glastonbury.

4) Saxon Stonework in the Church

Archeological digs in the summer of 2004 clearly showed that the settlement in Roman Shepton was not abandoned when the Romans left Britain. There is evidence of wooden structures with stone pads reusing the site and materials in the 5th century and very probably the 6th century. One burial on the site has been tentatively dated as 7th century. This suggestion of a Christian settlement in the fourth, fifth and sixth centuries at Fosse Lane combined with manuscript evidence of some sort of ecclesiastic at Sepetone in the seventh and eighth centuries, followed by significant Saxon remains in the Parish church, raise a tantalizing possibility of continuation.

There is believed to have been a small timber church on the site of the current church. According to local church historian Richard Rainsford, the church contains the most significant stone Saxon remains in Somerset. These can easily be spotted in the south wall of the nave by the chisel marks.

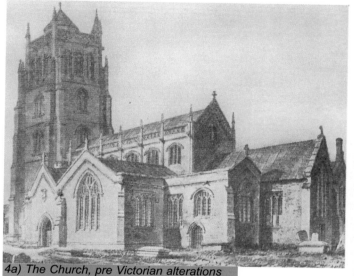

4a) The Church, pre Victorian alterations

4b) The Waggon ceiling

The parish church of St Peter and St Paul, a relatively unusual dual dedication, has evolved since then with each age leaving a development. It was extended and widened in the 12th century and the first tower built. In the 14th century a new tower was built encasing the first to become the 'earliest and finest of the Great Somerset Towers'. These were built with the wealth generated by the wool industry. Chewton Mendip and Leigh on Mendip are other fine examples of such church towers locally.

It is thought that the tower was originally designed to have a spire. On the roof of the tower is a distinctive five-sided cap that looks like the foundation for a spire. It is not thought to have ever been built though some suggest it may have been. In the late 15th century the roof was raised and replaced by a 'wagon roof'. The ceiling consisting of 350 carved panels each with a different design is one of the finest of its type in the whole country. It is hoped that lighting can be added to highlight this, one of the glories of the town.

As with most churches the church suffered at the hands of the Puritans, when many statues were removed or smashed. The nineteenth century also saw major alterations. The aisles were demolished and widened giving the current appearance of two rather flat roofed extensions. However it retains much to make it one of the finest churches of the county. For the millennium local stained glass artist, John Yeo, designed and installed a new stained glass window in the eastern end of the south aisle. Its striking contrast of colours provide a fitting celebration of at least 1,000 years' worship on the site.

To the north of the church stands the 'Old Grammar School' which until recently had been used as the rectory but is now a private house. This old building with its mullion windows is known to have

4c) Parish Church of St Peter and St Paul

dated from the early seventeenth century when George and William Strode founded the first Grammar School in 1627. It is probable that it is in fact a much older building and

5) Old Grammar School, by the Church

Farbrother, a former Headmaster, in his history of Shepton Mallet written in 1859, suggests that it was previously used as the Manor Court.

This started a long tradition of benefactors to the town, particularly by the Strode family. Edward Strode founded the Strode

6) Strode Alms Houses

almshouses which can be found on the south side of the churchyard. In 1699 He also made the original provision for the Bread Rooms charity which continued to give bread to the poor of the parish until the Second World War. People still alive can remember going to collect a 4lb charity loaf in the harsh depression of the 1930s. The almshouses are now run by Shepton United Charities which collected together all the old charities. The most eastern of the almshouses are those that date from the 17th century. The others date from the 19th Century together with those on the northeast side of the church. They still provide accommodation for the elderly of the parish.

The Bread Rooms have recently been taken over as the parochial parish office. Adjoining the Bread Rooms is No 8 Market Place. The only surviving example in the town of a fine 17th century town house of the sort a wealthy clothier would have then lived in. Over the past few years the owner has put a lot of effort into making the structure of the building sound and restoring it to its former glory.

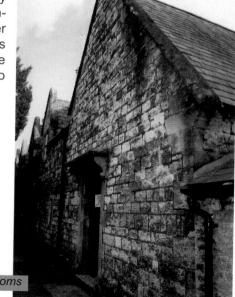

7) The Bread Rooms

Leg Square - into the valley - and the prison.

Shepton "lies in a steep-sided gully: the old streets are narrow and crooked; but the greater part of the town was built without regard to streets and the thoroughfares were made afterwards. Thus the town exists mostly of courts, alleys and isolated houses and the houses abut in all kinds of ways upon the lanes, some presenting their sides, others their backs and others again sticking out cornerwise."

8) The Prison circa 1920

So wrote local antiquarian Frank J Allen in Somerset Notes and Queries in 1888. The growing demands of the car and other transport during the 20th century saw roads increase conformity but in many areas of the valley it is possible still to picture the old town as described. Possibly this is best seen in the maze of lanes to the north and east of the church and leading down to Leg Square. Here there is an amazing jumble of stone walled alleyways, small labourers cottages alongside large and sometimes grand 18th century mill owners' 'manors'.

Dominating the area are the high sombre stonewalls of HM Prison. Now used to house 'lifers', the prison is the oldest surviving prison still used as such in the country. Frances Disney BEM has detailed many aspects of the Prison's history in the excellent 'Shepton Mallet Prison'. It was in 1625 that an acre of ground was purchased for a 'House of Correction and Bridewell for the benefit of the eastern part of the County.' The other two Somerset Prisons were at Ilchester and Taunton.

For over three centuries the prison acted as the 'House of Correction' for local misdemeanours. These ranged from highwaymen to witchcraft to religious dissent to poisoning to petty theft. Prisoners were held at the prison both before trial and after sentencing. In the days of harsh sentencing many received the ultimate punishment of death by hanging and there used to be a small graveyard to the east of the prison over what is now

Frithfield Lane. The name of this lane is interesting, until the 1930's it was called Gaol Lane. However local landowner Sir Frederick Berryman of Field House built a house at the top end of the lane for a former housekeeper. As he didn't like the idea of her living in 'Gaol Lane'; he used his position as Chairman of the Urban District Council to get it changed to Frithfield, the name of an adjoining field.

The prison has grown over the centuries. The traditional entrance off Town Lane is probably 18th century. There was significant extension during the 19th century which probably gave the form we are most familiar with now. The southwards extension is post-war.

Most recent interest in the prison has been in the role it played in the Second World War. The prison had shut for civil purposes in 1930. In 1939 the British Military took it over as a prison. The harsh regime that military prisoners endured is detailed in 'A Town Alive - Shepton Mallet 1939 - 45.' At the same time the former women's wing was being used by the Public Record Office to pro-

8a) The Prison's grand entrance

tect ancient documents from the bombing in London. The Magna Carta, the Domesday Book and various other precious documents were stored here for much of the war.

From 1942 the main part of the prison was taken over by the American Military for their miscreants. Unfortunately this included a number of murderers and rapists who received the death penalty and were executed inside the prison. Sixteen guilty prisoners were executed by hanging and two by firing squad. It is reputed that bullet marks can still be seen on the inside of the walls. The famous film the 'Dirty Dozen' took as a starting point the supposed terms of release of a group of American Prisoners from the Gaol to be given another chance to prove themselves in battle.

8b) The execution block at the prison

The Americans left following D Day in 1944 and the Prison returned to the British Military and as the 'Glasshouse', remained in use by them until the 1960s when it returned to civil use. There has been major investment in the prison since then and although not ideal, given the current shortage of prison places, it is expected to remain in use for a long time to come.

One fascinating thing about the prison is the acceptance of it by the town and even those living in the shadows of its walls. Its presence is just not an issue with the town, it has been there for centuries and there it sits with scarcely a comment.

Back down from the prison is the 'Leg Square' area of the town. The source of the name has been a matter of conjecture. Some feeling it was because the square was shaped like a leg. Old maps suggest this is unlikely. Leg was also an old Shepton family name however and it may be a question of which came first the family or the name. Old parchment documents show it being referred to as Leg Street right back to the 16th century. The name Leg Street was used in 19th century censuses.

There are three large mill owners' 'manors' which dominate the western end of the square. The Hollies, the gracious lines of the regency Edengrove - probably one of the most attractive houses in the town, and the Old Manor House. The Old Manor House is intriguing for the possibility that it could indeed be the ancient manor of Shepton Mallet. The use of the name 'Manor' for many large houses is a local eccentricity that can also be seen in neigbouring Croscombe. It makes it difficult to speculate accurately on past uses. The positioning of The Old Manor and that it adjoins 'Cornhill' could also be a contributory clue. It is a massive house whose wall show the scars of numerous alterations. Its eastern wing was used in the early 20th century as a hall for the Boys' Brigade.

Another feature of The Old Manor is at the Western end of its courtyard where there is

9) *Edengrove House, Leg Sq*

an excellent example of a rare 'spite wall'. If you go into Gaol Hill and look at the northern end of the first house on the left you will see that there are in fact two walls and in places it is still possible to see daylight between them. The outer wall belongs to The Old Manor and was built to ensure that their neighbour could not place a window with any view over the grounds of the Manor. The 1841 census lists a building here as 'No View Villa.' It was lived in by a family named Luff who were of independent means - a decided rarity for Shepton Mallet at that time. This family were local gentry in Stoney Stratton and Bowlish for much of the 20th century.

The fourth large building in this group is the former 'Town Mill' with its large chimney. It is now converted into flats and was previously owned by Showering who used it as a warehouse. Older inhabitants remember it as Virtue's Bakery which operated until after the Second World War. It was in this bakery that the Charity Loaves for distribution at

10) The Spite Wall, Leg Square

the Bread Rooms were baked. From the appearance of the building it is probable that it was originally a mill for grinding corn, probably both for flour and animal feed. Most of the

10a) Manor House, Leg Sq

11) Barrendown House

old Mills talked about in the town would have been for textile purposes.

Opposite the Town Mill behind tall trees and high walls are two large early 20th century houses. This was formally the site of the former Sherrin's 'Town Brewery.' All that remains of this brewery is the building just into Lower Lane on the right-hand side of the road. It is a comparatively recent conversion into a house. Previously it had been a Doctor's surgery. During the war it would seem to have been a dairy, part of Barren Down Farm. Prior to that it was supposed to have been a storehouse for the brewery and a dancing bear was reputed to have been caged there during its visits to the town. One look at the numerous alterations on the building's south wall along-side Lower Lane is enough to convince one that its history was a long and similarly varied one going back long before that.

Barrendown House behind this building has quite a grand look-ing early 19th century appear-ance. However documents going back before then suggest that it was artisans' houses that have been upgraded. This is a com-mon theme in Shepton Mallet where properties have been improved as wealth has allowed. It is one of a number of houses

11a) Much altered wall Lower Lane

which have connections with the Hyatt family. In this case going back at least to the 1790s when a Paul Hyatt who was a plumber and glazier was living there.

In the main part of Leg Square is one of Shepton Mallet's most famous public houses, the King's Arms, often known as the 'Dust Hole.' This name is reputed to have come from the dust on the workers' clothing from a quarry almost next door in Quarr. However it is just as likely to have been flour dust on the clothing of workers in the Town Mill. Examining census records shows that there used to be a lot more small cottages in this area. Looking at the King's Arms it is possible to see this. The eastern wing is on older maps shown as a number of small individual dwellings.

12) The Kings Arms (Dust Hole)

The Textile Heritage

The origin of the Shepton part of the name Shepton Mallet is always assumed to be derived from the Saxon for sheep farm 'Sceapton'. Surprisingly this is open to some dispute with some seeking the origin in the name of a Saxon lord and others suggesting an early religious, or even Roman origin 'Sepetone'. Given the prevalence of sheep throughout this pastoral area of the country and their even greater numbers in the Cotswolds, Chilterns and East Anglia it would seem surprising if a small settlement in Somerset was one of a very few places in the country to be named after a very common creature.

What is not in doubt is the fact that the development of the town in the mediaeval period was derived from wool and its processing into cloth. The period of great wealth of the town through the 17th and 18th centeries was born out of the profits derived by merchants from an estimated 4,000 people working either in cottages or mills at spinning and weaving wool into cloth.

A number of the wealthy merchants' 'Manor Houses' survive as seen in Leg Square and also in Bowlish and other spots along the valley bottom. A fair number of the small textile workers' cottages also survive, Garston Street being the best example. However the evidence of the woollen mills appears quite thin on the ground until closer examination is made.

13) Bowlish House

It is alleged that at one time there were more than thirty mills powered by the rather insignificant river which runs along the valley and its even smaller tributaries. When given a name at all this stream was probably 'Doulting Water' or the River Brae until the Ordnance Survey map-makers grandly labeled it as 'The River Sheppey' in the late 19th

14) Mill Races, Darshill

century. A walk along the river in summer can make you wonder if there is enough water to power one mill. However there was a complex arrangement of leats, races and millponds to build up a 'head' of water. A walk along the Wells road from Bowlish to Darshill peering over the wall and into gardens is perhaps the best place to see this. It is sometimes difficult to be sure which is the stream and which is mill leat or race.

Although it is suggested there were at least 30 mills, sites for nowhere near this number have been located. The industry entered decay from about the beginning of the 19th century and although some element of the textile industry kept going until the beginning of the 20th century it was a process of long gradual decline. The huge ruins of two of the most prominent textile mills were demolished in the 1970s.

Today the last significant recognizable 18th century mill is probably the Silk Mill in Coombe Lane up the steep narrow valley that comes into the Sheppey at Bowlish. This

15) Converted Mill, Coombe Lane

attractive building has been well converted into houses and flats and its conversion has rejuvenated the lane. Of the small tributary which one powered the mill there seems no sign as it has been fully piped under Combe Lane. It is difficult to imagine a stream powerful enough to run an industrial-scale factory: unless you stand at the top of Coombe Lane just after a heavy shower. The powerful sound of roaring in the drains reveals a stream of considerable force.

In Darshill there were originally at least three mills - an upper mill, possibly two middle mills, and a lower mill are recorded. The 'lower mill' is now under the sewage farm which was built in the mid 19th century. Some of the stonework behind it may be from the old mill. Coming back up the stream is what is now called Silk Mills. The main building appears to be late 19th century and is not very mill-like in appearance. However it could be a rebuilding of an early small mill. It is speculated that the strange aerated brick barn

16) Silk Mills, Wells Road

outbuilding next to the road was used for the drying of teasels used in raising the knap on cloth.

The main 'Middle Mill' was at the head of the long overgrown millpond that runs alongside the main road. And there, sure enough, is a building which appears in the style of an old mill. Locals of course will know that this was only built in 2000. It is however on the site of what was a much larger mill building which was the major employer in the west end of the town making silk in the middle of the 19th century.

The 1841 census shows a large number of textile workers in Darshill and Bowlish. The list includes many silk winders, silk throwsters and silk weavers plus also crape weavers, silk packers, silk twisters, velvet weavers, silk quillers, powerloom weavers, dyers, loom overlooker and various engineers who were probably associated with the mills.

In other parts of the town too it is possible to see other remains of the once mighty textile industry. The award-winning industrial estate at the eastern end of town is in the main

17) Not what it appears - New houses at Darshill

17a) The original Middle Mill Darshill

an attractive conversion of the Charlton Brewery. However the western block of buildings was a former woollen mill dating back at least to the 17th century. The mill pond for holding up the head of water is still very much a feature of the site and the name Ticklebelly Lane and Ticklebelly Cottage is believed to have a textile working origin, though a Saxon derivation has also been suggested.

In Kilver Street what is now the headquarters of the Mulberry Fashion empire was at the beginning of the twentieth century 'Jardine's Factory'. This factory was rebuilt on the site of a mill which had been destroyed by fire in the 1850s. In the first decade of the 20th

18) Jardines Mill, now Mulberry Head Quarters

century it was bought by a Nottingham company Jardine's. Ernest Jardine moved to the area to further his political career but proved an enlightened employer. He provided gardens for staff to take recreation in and allotments for them to grow vegetables. The gardens were later further developed to become the gorgeous Babycham gardens which can be seen through a gate way in the lane to the south of the factory, and are occasionally opened to the public. The lake in the garden is, of course, another millpond and the sluice controls are still in operation. The factory shut in the inter-war period. During the war it was taken over by the National Deposit Friendly Society which moved out of London for the duration. After the war it was refitted to become the luxurious head office for the Showerings empire which, with the success of 'Babycham', became a major employer in the 1950s and 60s.

The causes of the decline of Shepton Mallet's woollen industry during the 19th century would seem to be complex. It was a decline matched throughout the Cotswold Woollen manufacturing area of which Shepton Mallet and Frome were considered the southern boundary. From the middle of the 18th century a feature of the industrial revolution had been the emergence of the huge 'dark satanic mills' of Lancashire and Yorkshire where first water power and then steam power drove machinery of ever increasing size and complexity. In the economic recession after the end of the Napoleonic wars their cost advantages probably squeezed this area out of the market. In Shepton Mallet we were only five miles from the nearest coalmines, 19th century censuses even show a few colliers living in the town. However no very large mills harnessing coal power were built. Perhaps it was the topography of steep little valleys which limited the space for large mills. Probably the decline was contributed to by the wealthy local merchants who may not have had the entrepreneurial ambition to match the achievements of the new breed of northern industrialists.

19) Old Mill at Charlton Brewery site

It is also possible that the attitude of local textile workers contributed to the decline. Always a rebellious town, in 1776 Shepton Mallet was the scene of some of the first industrial unrest in the country against the introduction of machinery such as the 'spinning jenny' which mechanized the jobs of workers. According to a local paper ' a riotous mob of weavers and shear-men collected from the towns of Warminster, Frome and other areas.......proceeded to the town of Shepton Mallet, with an intent to destroy...a spinning machine lately erected by the clothiers...and to pull down houses...'

In the riot that ensued the military were called out and in the struggle to control the situation one of the rioters was killed. The riot was said to have taken place on 'Bunker Hill' which is claimed to be the site of the Norah Fry Hospital. This sort of riot and smashing of machinery later built into the infamous 'Luddite Movement' which caused so much havoc in the early part of the 19th century. It is one of Shepton Mallet's less known claims to fame that it may well have had its origins here.

Garston Street

Sheptonians born before the war, when asked where they come from, will frequently respond, 'Kilver Street', or 'Draycott', or 'Darshill' and especially 'Garston Street.' They are living testament to the tradition that Shepton Mallet was a string of separate communities along the bottom of the valley, each with a separate identity, with the 'town' around the Market Square up the hill to the south. Early maps show little of the town outside the valley floor with the exception of the area around the Market Square and Church.

Redevelopment and road widening, mainly since the Second World War, has wiped away much of the network of separate communities. Draycott was decimated by the 'progressive' improvement that was to become the Hillmead development which had to be significantly redeveloped itself after only 20 years. There is almost nothing left of the community which was Kilver Street. Sixty years ago it had many cottages, pubs, a school, shops and a slaughterhouse. Now it is just a wide main road with the Gaymer's Cider factory on one side and the Mulberrry fashion accessory company head office and shop on the other.

Garston Street is the best example of what is left, though much changed from days past. That it survives at all is down to the efforts of Dr Alan Blandford and the Shepton Mallet Amenity Trust that he founded in the 1960s. Showerings were hoping to get Garston Street demolished to extend their factory which had already swallowed Prospect Place and so much of the other local land and cottages. The Amenity Trust fought this and bought and restored some of the cottages which had fallen into disrepair. We have been left with a marvellous long line of varied cottages which are a standing monument to much of Shepton Mallet's history.

20) Cottages in Garston Street

20a) Weavers cottages, Garston St

Garston Street resident Roger Male and his daughter Trudy have been investigating the history of Garston Street for many years and it is hoped that their studies will one day see the light of day. Roger has deeds for his house going back to the 1600s and it is probable that many of the buildings in the long row date from soon after then, though many have been built and rebuilt, or at least refronted since then. There is a wealth of styles, a

20b) Former 'White Hart' pub, Garston Street

20c) Raised pavement level and old doorways, Garston St

study of the window frames ranges from mullions to sashes to some interesting ornate variations. With a little investigation the site of a pub which shut in the 1970s and a shop which shut in the 1980s can be spotted. Other shops, at least two bakeries and a 19th century Baptist chapel can also be spotted.

Some of the cottages are three stories high, the top story with windows to let in light for the weavers who used to work in their homes. It is probable that some of these top stories originally ran over two or more houses. In many houses it can be seen that the ground floor windows are very low to the street showing where road levels have been built up over the years.

It is also interesting to see the mix in status of the houses. Although all houses adjoin, it can be seen that, although most are simple artisans' dwellings there are others of a higher status. Merchants, traders and professionals living in amongst the textile workers.

This is very much the picture that can be seen in the 1841 census. The population of Garston Street, Quarr and the now vanished New Street and Prospect Place was approximately 500 - a sizeable 'village' in its own right for those days. The vast majority were labourers and textile workers but it also included many tradesmen and craftsmen including a sawyer, shoemakers, plumbers, a plasterer, shopkeepers, stonemasons, a butcher, a cooper, a governess, a school teacher, a tea dealer, a thatcher, tailors, straw bonnet makers, a grocer, a dressmaker, an engineer toolmaker, and gardeners.

Old inhabitants best remember the community spirit. The road passed right in front of the small houses, and in days when the motor car remained a rarity, children used to play out in the street and the women would come out into the street to gossip and hang up their washing. The huge factory which now so dominates the south side of the road did not exist then and there were gardens running down towards the river. It is still possible to identify a few brick buildings on the south side of the road which are used as sheds but before that as the outdoor lavatories.

A local farmer can remember that before the war when his father needed help with hay making of an evening he would drive down to Garston Street. The men would be outside talking or gardening and in those days of economic hardship, he just had to call out to round up a gang for a few hours work getting the hay in from a field.

Although much has changed and there are now no shops, there still seems to be a sense of community in Garston Street. When leading history walks down there local residents always come out to talk to people about their street. If former residents are present there is always chatter about 'do you remember so and so?' In today's society when so few people know their neighbours it is refreshing to see that the Garston Street spirit is maintained.

20d) Another view of Garston Street

Education in Shepton Mallet

Shepton is not noted as a great educational town in the way that Bruton or Sherborne have been with their selection of schools. However education in Shepton Mallet has a long and varied tradition.

5a) The Old Grammar School 1859

The Old Grammar School was founded by an endowment from the Strode family in 1627 on the north side of the church-yard. The initial endowment was for the teaching of 12 scholars but it also included almshouses for 5 women. This arrangement seems to have continued for 150 years until it was deemed unsuitable. The school would appear to have had its ups and downs falling on one occasion into an almost ruinous state. The problem seems to have been that the masters received the value of the endowment and some were interested more in the money than the job. It reached its worst when, in the late 18th century, the son of the previous incumbent claimed it was his hereditary right.

The school picked up in the early 19th century when, for about 20 years it was reputed as being **the** school for the local gentry to send their son to. Again in the mid century under the headship of John Farbrother, Shepton Mallet's first historian, it gained an excellent reputation. The school was extended into what we now know as the St Peter Street Rooms.

21) The former Grammar School 1900s (now leisure centre)

Around 1900 a new Grammar School was built along Charlton Road. It again had an excellent name and many of the local farmers sent their sons there. Reports still exist of the enlightened educational work undertaken there including testing of milk quality and the effects of fertilizers on crop yields. Sadly county educational authorities didn't seem to think that Shepton Mallet justified a Grammar school and it was shut during the 1920s. Scholarship pupils were sent either to Sexey's, for boys, or Sunnyhill, for girls, in Bruton or the Blue school in Wells. The buildings were still used for metal work, cookery and science labs for the Senior Schools some distance away in Waterloo Road. This continued until the building of Whitstone School in the 1960s and 70s. The Grammar School buildings are now used as the Sports and Leisure centre.

Before the beginning of state education in the second half of the 19th Century, there were a number of small, privately run schools in Shepton Mallet. Each would probably have had fewer than 20 pupils and be run as a private business by the teacher, many of them deserving the description 'Dame Schools'. Pigot & Co's Directory for 1830 lists the following 'Academies' in the town:

Baker and Richmond (ladies') Draycott;
Sarah Bartlett, Town's End;
Francis Byrt, Paul Street;
Fanny Cooper, Slade's Close;
Miss Driver, Harridge House;
Sarah Glover, Croscombe;
Robert Norton, High Street;
Lydia Smith, Broadway, Paul Street;
John Vickery, Draycott.

The 1841 census shows that at that time Bowlish House, presumably deprived of wealthy mill owners, was being used as a girls school.

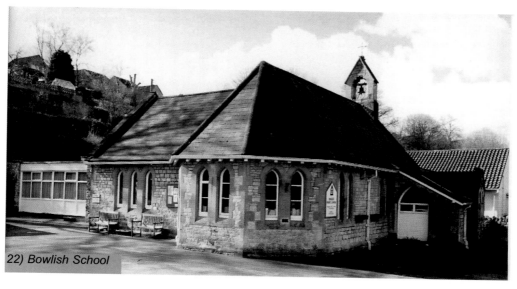

22) Bowlish School

31

The town's Methodist chapels also each had their own schoolrooms. The buildings behind the Methodist Chapel and the Baptist Chapel both show extensive building for this purpose, though in later years they would have just been Sunday schools. Just think, it is probably less than 50 years ago that it would have been accepted that the majority of children would attend a Sunday school. There was also a school attached to the workhouse on Old Wells Road.

In the second half of the 19th Century the three original state-funded schools were built when the principle of education for all was established. When Bowlish School first opened in 1869 it provided an interesting addition to the area. Not only did it provide education for the children of workers in the nearby mills but it also provided a place of worship. Every Sunday there was a service at 6.30pm. As the Shepton Mallet Journal reported on its Centenary, ' When the Church Service was over, the floor boards would hinge, and by a complexity of ropes and pulleys, a partition was raised to protect the altar from the coarser language and frequent missiles of the workhouse and mill children.'

Some of this working mechanism turned up in the 1990s when the floor had to be replaced and the cellars, prone to flooding from the nearby River Sheppey, were filled in. Nowadays Bowlish is an excellent Infant school with around 100 children from the age of 4 - 7 who are looked after in four classrooms. Originally it looked after around 120 children in two classrooms from the ages of 4 to 12 when they left school. In the 1920s the opening of the Senior schools allowed this to be reduced to 4 - 11 year olds which it continued teaching until the 1970s when St Paul's Junior School was opened.

Along with Bowlish the other two late 19th century state schools were Kilver Street and

22a) Bowlish in its valley

BOWLISH, SHEPTON MALLET.

23) Shepton Mallet Infants circa 1900

NEW INFANTS SCHOOL, WATERLOO ROAD, SHEPTON MALLET.

Waterloo Road. Both buildings are immediately recognizable as schools from their distinctive style. Each served their local community along the valley bottom. Waterloo Road on the north side of the valley with its views over the town is still very much in business as Shepton Mallet Infant School, the young children dressed in blue sweatshirts as against the red of Bowlish. Sadly Kilver Street is no longer a school, though many local residents remember when it was. Subsequently it was used as offices for Showerings for

24) Kilver Street School, now Mulberry's Factory Shop

25) Former Senior School, Waterloo Road

many years but now serves as the high class 'factory' shop for the Mulberry company with their top of the market range of clothes and furnishing in distinctive textiles.

Between the wars, in response to growing need, two "Senior' schools were built higher up Waterloo Road. These have now long been converted into old peoples flats and many local residents have totally forgotten the buildings original use. Recently I was contacted by someone who knew she had moved into the old school house but wasn't sure where the school had been.

On one site, the school was split in two, a boys school and a girls school each with its

23a) Shepton Mallet Infants, Waterloo Rd

26) Whitstone -serving the community

own head and operating separately. It would seem that from the start they had been built too small with pupils having to walk a few hundred yards to the former Grammar School buildings for science and craft lessons. As war began in 1939 the county council completed the purchase of Whitstone Park - next to the Grammar School in Charlton Road - for the building of a new secondary school for the town. However it was a quarter of a century before work was begun. Whitstone School was built in stages to a modern design. For some years classes continued to be spread around the town including some in the old Methodist Chapel rooms.

Whitstone School, when built, was well equipped and popular. It had a strong Rural Studies section and many teachers have spent fruitful careers there, a number teaching more than one generation of Shepton children. However education moved on, Rural Studies was deemed an irrelevancy to modern needs, the school leaving age was raised to 16 and then with much focus on sixth form and further education, a number of parents considered Strode College, eleven miles distant in Street, was not what they wanted for their sixteen year olds and sent their children, at age eleven, to the Blue School in Wells where there was a sixth form. In particular fewer children were coming into Whitstone from the local villages. By the early 1990s numbers were close to falling below 500 and as one of the smallest secondary schools in Somerset there were rumours as to its possi-

26a) Whitstone , serving the community

ble future, or lack of one. Then Steve Chaudoir arrived as head master and began a remarkable transformation. Standards have risen, pupil numbers are now over 700, the school is an Information Technology college and, including management of the leisure centre, provides a vital and active role for the local community.

Small private schools continued to be in evidence in the 20th century. Right through the Second World War the local newspaper regularly contained advertisements for both the Ivy House School and the Saviour Convent.

"The Ivy House School for Girls, preparatory school for boys, principal Miss Edis. Special classes for elocution, dancing, dalcrouage, eurhythmics, shorthand, book-keeping."

"Saviour Convent, boarding and day school for girls and small boys. The course of instruction includes the usual English subjects, also French, drawing, painting, class singing, needlework, drill and dancing."

27) Langhorne House, former convent now St Paul's School

The convent continued until the 1960s and was run by an order of nuns who had a base in the town including the house which is now Bartlett and Co Solicitors in the High Street. The school was based in the magnificent Langhorne House and park in Paul Street. The house was built in the mid 19th century and in the late 19th century it was one of the houses lived in by the Garton family when they ran the Anglo Bavarian Brewery.

When in the 1970s education in Shepton was reorganized, Bowlish and Waterloo Road became the town's infant schools and the former convent became St Paul's Junior School for children between 7 and 11 from where they would go up to Whitstone. Already equipped with a magnificent school hall, the buildings were extended and improved and parental effort added a swimming pool. Some may not consider the buildings ideal for a modern school but it is certainly better equipped than most schools that pupils of that age group find in smaller village primary schools. The parkland setting is also excellent and traces of former formal gardens survive. For me, a Shepton Mallet highlight was the summer concert when my children were at the school. A fine summer's evening with chairs in a wide spread semi-circle on the lawn with the young musicians gallantly performing against a back-drop of the fine wisteria-clad south front of Langhorne House.

27a) The tranquil rear view of St Paul's School

Hospitals

Medical care in the town has a long history. The Pigot and Co's Directory for 1830 lists the following 'surgeons':

Geo Frederick Burroughs, Paul Street;
John Edgar, Cornhill;
Alfred Gale, High Street;
William Grist, Peter Street;
Philip Marshall, Longbridge;
John Mines, High Street.

There were also two 'Chymists & Druggists', Robert Bartlett, High Street; and John Young, High Street. However for the first evidence of a hospital we need to look to 1869 and the opening of Shepton Mallet District Hospital.

28) Shepton Mallet District Hospital 1880's

The year before, the long-serving Dr Craddock proposed a hospital. A public meeting was held at the 'Music Hall' in 1868 and a fund started. Local patrons included Major Paget of Cranmore Hall, the local MP. Donations from the local gentry combined with the revenue of a concert and a bazaar built up a healthy fund. The house in Waterloo Road which had been lived in by Dr

28a) Former Shepton Mallet District Hospital

Craddock was bought and converted as a hospital which could house 12 in-patients. The professional medical staff gave their time free of charge to the hospital and these are listed as Dr Wybrants, consulting physician, and Drs Craddock, Smith and J. T. Hyatt.

In 1879 it was decided to build a new purpose-designed Hospital and a site was purchased from the Duchy of Cornwall on the edge of Barren Down. After a keen competition from 17 applicants, an architect from Norwich was commissioned to design the building and local builder Messrs J & S Emery to build it. It eventually cost over £2,000 which included laying out Princes Road. Once the foundations where set there was a brick laying ceremony following a procession through the town. Over 5,000 people were reputed to have watched a young Mrs. Paget, wife of Major Paget, lay a foundation stone with a silver trowel made especially for the occasion. The association of the Pagets with the hospital was long. At the 75th anniversary the Mrs. Paget of the day said that her mother-in-law, by then in her late nineties, was unable to attend but still took a lively interest in the business of the hospital.

This hospital continued to serve the town until the late 1990s and has since been attractively turned into flats. Fortunately, unlike many other hospitals of the period it has not suffered the fate of demolition and the gothic shape of the building is still instantly recognizable as that of the original building.

The hospital with the biggest physical presence in the town is certainly the Norah Fry at Westend in West Shepton. This was for a long time the local workhouse. From Elizabethan times the looking after the poor of the parish had been the responsibility of the local parish and as the local ratepayers had to pay for it, it can be imagined that the amount of money spent was often a contentious issue. In 1835 an Act was passed in parliament allowing parishes to join together to act in 'Union's' of parishes. There was also a corresponding move away from a tradition of out relief to a philosophy of Workhouses.

29) Norah Fry Hospital, undergoing conversion to residential

29a) Norah Fry, last days as a hospital 1990s

A belief was prevelant, amongst the politically influencial, that the poor were poor because of their own lack of effort and if they were housed in grim workhouse institutions they would soon try harder not to be a burden on the rate payers. It might have been obvious that this was never going to work for the elderly and the infirm, but perhaps it was economic expediency that drove it after all.

In 1836 Shepton Mallet and the surrounding parishes significantly enlarged an existing workhouse at Westend and the plans show that this building had much of the footprint of the later 1848 further enlargement and enhancing which is basically what we see today. A local architect, Jesse Gane, was heavily involved in both phases as were local Surveyors Wainwright's who remained in the town for nearly 150 years.

Already by 1841 the census showed the workhouse had around 140 paupers in residence. The master is shown as James Cogle and his wife Sarah is matron. Jane Satchell is listed as Schoolmistress - presumably to provide some sort of help for the many children. There were also around a dozen paupers aged 70-plus being subjected to the harsh regime. As time went by the Workhouse would have added some health care elements. There were also eight tramps cells. The tramps' would be required to break a load of stone for road building in return for their night's keep. Many tramps would wander the countryside passing from workhouse to workhouse.

It was only shortly before the First World War that old age pensions were first introduced - a realization that poverty in old age needed a different approach. It was not until the

1920s that the workhouse ethos became fully redundant and, even now, the idea of shame in poverty is still strong in our western society. In 1930 the workhouse and its infirmary came under the control of Somerset County Council as a home for the mentally ill. Many mentally infirm people had previously been treated as paupers and were victims of the workhouse regime. It was under the supervision of the remarkable Miss Norah Fry, who was involved in the hospital for the next 30 years, that the considerable improvement in the conditions for patients and the introduction of specialist nursing staff took place. In 1947 the hospital became part of the National Health Service and was known as West End House. Miss Fry seems to have been a fascinating person. She came from a prominent Somerset family. In 1918 she became the first female county councillor and in 1932, an Alderman. When the elderly Norah Fry died, aged ninety, in 1960 the hospital was renamed in her honour.

Attitudes towards mental illness advanced during the last quarter of the 20th century and large institutions became frowned upon as 'care in the community' became the buzzwords. The former staff building on the opposite side of the Old Wells Road has been converted to become one of a number of hostels around the town and there is also a modern day centre just behind this. The Norah Fry Hospital finally closed in 1993 and a decade of neglect and vandalism followed while the district council procrastinated over what they wanted to do with it. Finally in 2004 work started on an ambitious restoration and conversion scheme, turning the former workhouse buildings into houses and apartments.

30) St Peter's Community Hospital

Other than hostels and nursing homes, hospital activity in Shepton is now focused on the St Peter's Community Hospital site on the western edge of the town. This had originally begun life in the inter-war period as an isolation hospital. In pre-antibiotic days, when consumption (TB), scarlet fever and diphtheria all required infectious patients to be isolated

31) Former isolation unit, Waterloo Road

for considerable periods, there were a number of isolation units. Sites known include the buildings to the north of the Norah Fry and the first building on the left past the viaduct going north up Waterloo Road. When first built, St Peter's Hospital truly was isolated, well away from others. It was reached down the narrow winding Bowlish Lane which ran from the Old Wells Road to Bowlish. Its route can still be traced as a footpath running through the St Peter's Estate. As late as the Second World War the Shepton Mallet Urban District Council was arguing that it didn't need to maintain this lane. A compromise had to be reached with the hospital having to pay 50% of the cost of surfacing the road, and then it was only surfaced as far as the hospital itself.

In the days of the National Health Service an excellent Maternity unit has been provided though it has come under repeated threats of closure. Since the closure of the Shepton Mallet District Hospital in the early 1990s, St Peter's hospital has been expanded and an excellent range of Out Patients' services added. 2004 saw the start on building an additional private hospital on the site promising rapid American-style operations to cut National Health service waiting times. Its striking appearance seems sadly out of place and to have been modeled on an inverted empty ice-cream container or margarine tub.

30a) New Hospital at St Peter's

The Non-Conformists

Shepton Mallet is one of many West Country towns with a long association with non-conformist religions. It is possible this dissent dates back to the 16th century as cloth merchants and skilled textile workers such as the Huguenots in France were at the forefront of 'Protestantism'. Their beliefs may well have spread to the woollen industry in the west. Certainly in the 17th century Shepton Mallet was seen to side with the Parliamentarians and then with the Duke of Monmouth.

In the 19th century there would appear to have been an element of truth in the generalization that the gentry and land owners went to church, the traders and skilled workers went to chapel, whilst the workers went to one or the other. A wide range of places to worship grew up. These have left us with some of the finest 18th and 19th century buildings in the town, though unfortunately these are sometimes buildings which struggle to find a suitable role in today's world.

A directory of the town published in 1930 by Clare's of Wells sets out the options for religious worship. As well as the Parish Church of St Peter and St Paul, the Roman Catholic Church in West Shepton and the Gospel Hall in Board Cross, four non conformist chapels are listed.

'The Baptist Church, Commercial Road, Shepton Mallet. Minister -Pastor F L Hawkins, 46 West Shepton. Divine service - Sunday 11am, 6pm. Tuesdays, 7.30pm. Sunday school and Children's Service - Sundays 2.30pm. Women's meeting, Wednesdays, 3 pm.'

The Baptist church was in fact the most recent to establish itself in Shepton Mallet. During the 1980s, Church Secretary Bill Biles wrote a series of short articles on local Baptist his-

32) The former 'Iron Chapel,' Commercial Road

tory. These were turned into a pamphlet in 2001. In 1858 it was decided to purchase a house in Garston Street and until 1875, services were held there under the auspices of the Baptist Church of Wells. In 1875 they broke away from Wells and had a joint Pastor with Croscombe and North Wootton. The house in Garston Street was converted into a chapel and had a new front built. This building is still easily spotted in the middle of the long rank of building in Garston Sreet. This ceased to be used in 1895 and was later sold off and became a bakery and is now a private residence.

20e) Former Baptist Chapel, Garston St.

Religious differences within the group led to them moving to the Congregational Iron Chapel in Commercial Road, which became the Baptist Church. This is now a workshop for a firm of shop fitters. In 1966 the Baptists bought the Congregational (Independent) Church in Commercial Road where they are still very active within the town.

'Congregational Church' Commercial Road Minister --. Divine Service - Sundays,

33) Congregational Church (now Baptist) Commercial Road

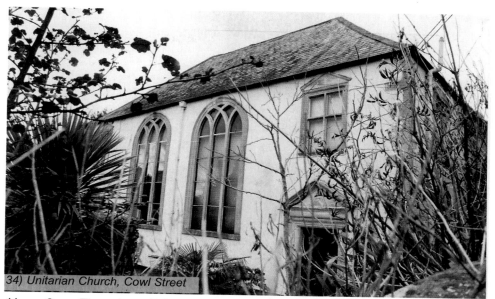
34) Unitarian Church, Cowl Street

11am, 6pm. Thursdays, 7.30pm. Union of Young Worshippers, Sundays 11am. Sunday School 2.15pm.'

This was long known as the Independent 'Hephzibah' Chapel. It was founded in 1801 although Farbrother says there was a Sunday school 'in connection with this cause' opened in Bowlish in 1798. The Chapel was originally built in 1801 and was significantly enlarged in 1814 to hold 700 people. There were quite extensive school buildings attached to it's south end.

In 1966 the building was sold to the Baptist Church who, despite the problems with falling congregations faced by all churches, now seem to have become one of the more buoyant churches in the town. The building is one of the town's lesser known treasures and is grade 2 listed both inside and out. It is probably over familiarity with Methodist Chapels which leads to us scarcely noticing their impressive facades. Inside however this Chapel is a delight, retaining its original balcony and woodwork. You are immediately transported back into the atmosphere of the nineteenth century. Imagine services, which would have had many hundred worshipers present, the organ leading the singing of solemn hymns and the Minister delivering a fire and brimstone sermon.

'**Unitarian Church**, Cowl Street, Founded 1692. Minister - Rev H E Haycock, 7 Westfield. Divine Worship, 6pm Sunday School 2,30pm.'

The oldest and, externally, probably the finest of the major Chapel buildings in Shepton Mallet, the Unitarian Chapel in Cowl Street, was built in 1692 and enlarged in 1758. It is now converted into three private residences. It formally had a burial ground and according to inhabitants odd bones have been known to turn up during gardening. This Chapel also has a schoolroom to the rear. It used to contain a fine oak carved canopied pulpit but what became of this no one seems to know.

'**Wesleyan Church**, Paul Street. Resident Minister Rev G H Schofield, Centenary House. Sunday Services, Morning 11; evening, 6: Sunday School, Morning, 10.15; Afternoon 2.15pm. Weeknight Service, Alternate Tuesdays 7.30pm. Minister's Class, Alternate Tuesdays 7.30pm. Wesley Guild Thursdays 7.30pm (October to April.) Women's Meeting, Tuesdays 3 pm. Ladies Sewing Guild, Wednesdays 3 pm (October to April.) Choir Practice, Fridays 8pm.'

The imposing 'Ebenezer' chapel in Paul Street was built in 1819 when the Chapel, with by then 176 members, bought the site of the former Tennis Court Inn. This name is

35) former interior Methodist Church

intriguing in itself, the lawn tennis we know today was not invented until the late nineteenth century. In the eighteenth century tennis was associated with the gambling and Pubs. Presumably this court would have more resembled a 'Real Tennis' court, a game identified with public schools, more akin to squash.

It is thought that this chapel was the third Chapel of the Wesleyans in Shepton Mallet. Records suggest a previous one in Park Road built in 1772. John Wesley himself preached in the town on a number of occasions between 1746 and 1790. In 1748 a hired mob was organized to attack him.

35a) former Methodist Church, Paul Street

The Chapel itself was the biggest in the town and was supposed to be able to hold 1,000 people. It also formally included a balcony and organ but was later altered to two floors. Like the other major chapels it has extensive schoolrooms to the rear. The chapel was shut in the 1990s, the Methodists since then holding services in the Parish Church. Under

35b) The porch, former Methodist Church

private ownership the Chapel has since been run as a community centre used by a number of local organizations.

Other Religious buildings

With the earliest evidence of Christianity in the west country - the Chi-Rho Amulet, the most significant Saxon stone church remains in Somerset, a parish church with the finest waggon roof in the country and a tower rated as one of the best in the county; plus a wonderful selection of non conformist chapels it is a shame that the claims of Glastonbury and Wells with their mere ruined Abbey and Catherdral respectively have been allowed to over-shadow Shepton Mallet in the religious tourists eyes.

However, even yet we have not seen the full extent of religious gems. Other religious buildings in the town include the former Roman Catholic Church in West Shepton built in 1804. This was very early for the setting up of a Roman Catholic parish church following nearly two centuries when 'papism' had been considered a threat to the country and Roman Catholics had had to worship in semi secret. It is interesting to see it re-establishing itself in a town which appears to have had a wide variety of religions and therefore probably a good degree of religious tolerance. The unusual gothic style church has now been converted to private accomodation and will sit strangely amidst the redevelopment of the former Clarks factory site into a retail complex. The current Roman Catholic Church

36) The former R.C. Church, Townsend

in Park Road was built in the modern style during the 1970's following a generous anonomous bequest.

There have at times been various orderes of nuns in the town, the magnificent Sales House in Draycott was the home of an order up until the 1830's when they moved to Westbury on Trym in Bristol. The nuns who ran the convent St Saviours Convent School in Langhorne House also occupied the fine house in the High Street which is now occupied by solicitors Bartlett Gooding and Weelan. Some former pupils of the school living

37) The Roman Catholic Church, Park Road

locally who are still in touch with the last of the elderly nuns who were their former teachers.

A former Church/ Church room can be seen Cannard's Grave which was active up to the Second World War and beyond. The local farming family the Normans were very involved in the running of this small church. During the war it was the scene of many well attended fund raising whist drives, a formally very popular form of entertainment which has faded away in recent decades. There was also a Methodist Meeting House in Downside (now demolished.) The Salvation Army is believed to have started in Draycott, moved to Board Cross and then in the last few years has moved to the town's former

38) Sales House, Draycott, before restoration in 1980's

39) former Magistrates court now Salvation Army Gospel Hall, Commercial Rd

Magistrates Court in Commercial Road.

The town cemetery over the bridge from Waterloo road has a splendid late 19th Century pair of matching Mortuary Chapels that many architectural historians have commented on favourably. The cemetery was founded in the mid 19th Century and has a number of fine monuments. Its maintainance is a constant head ache to the town council.

The fascinating subject of the history of religious movements in Shepton Mallet is worthy of a much deeper study than that offered here.

40) Mortuary Chapels in cemetery, Waterloo Road

Beer

From the early years of the 19th century the textile industry, which for so long had provided the backbone of the local economy, entered a long and painful decline. From being a wealthy town Shepton quickly began to show signs of poverty. Into the void left by textiles new industries began to grow and prime amongst these was probably the brewing industry which lasted until well into the 20th century. Some of the largest and most prominent buildings in Shepton Mallet are related to these breweries.

Up until the 19th century, pubs would usually have had their own brew house. In fact many households would have brewed their own beer and most farms made their own cider. Gradually production became focused into more specialized units and commercial breweries started to grow up producing more consistent and distinctive brews for local pubs or other markets.

Probably the first of these specialized breweries and maltings in Shepton Mallet was that set up in Oakhill by Jordan and Billingsley in the 1760s using the favoured waters from Mendip springs. Oakhill at that time was the northern part of the Shepton Mallet Parish and the village itself only initially developed to house and serve the brewery workers. As it now counts as a separate village, Oakhill is really outside the scope of this study.

In Shepton the first major brewery recorded is the Old Town Brewery in Leg Street (Now referred to as Leg Square). This was probably founded and run by one of the innumerable Hyatts who were so prominent in Shepton Mallet for so long. It is known that they were living in adjacent properties in the 1800s and the Pigot and Co Directory for 1830 lists under Brewers, Thomas Hyatt, Leg Street. This brewery was later known as Sherrin's brewery. It ran until the early years of the 20th century but was then demolished and two fine detached houses built on the site.

19a) Brewers House and Brewery Buildings, Charlton Brewery

The next of the bigger breweries to be founded was the
Charlton Brewery and Maltings
founded in 1844 by Frederick
Berryman, largely taking over
the site of a former woollen mill
deep in the valley at the eastern
end of town. This grew to be a
major business supplying many
pubs over an extensive area
around Shepton. By the 20th
century the Berryman's had
become the local 'gentry' living
in Field House to the south of
the town. The then Sir
Frederick Berryman was prominent on the town council for
over 50 years and was, in the
1930s, the Chairman of
Somerset County Council. The
brewery was then run by
Charles Burnell who lived at
Charlton House and also
became one of the most prominent local citizens.

There are still people around who worked at the brewery and many others remember
items such as their two steam wagons which were used for deliveries of beer up until the

19b) Charlton Brewery and mill pond, before restoration

Second World War made it impossible to find spares.

After the war the brewery was taken over by Georges of Bristol and then the mighty Courage empire and gradually closed down. The site was eventually taken over by local developer Dennis Dennett and his wife Sue. From the mid 1980s they set about developing the massive range of buildings in a most enlightened way into a business park. Focused around the old millpond the site now houses companies ranging from engineering to software and internet, to an art gallery. New buildings have been added to blend into the attractive historic surroundings and the whole has become an excellent example of the best way redundant buildings can be found new life.

19c) Mill Pond, Charlton Brewery

The most prominent of the 19th century breweries is without doubt the Anglo Bavarian Brewery built on the crest of the hill on the south side of the valley. The massive ornate frontage still dominates many views of the town in the same way as breweries such as Wadsworths at Devizes or Hall and Woodhouse at Blandford. According to an excellent account by Alfred Barnard,

41) The Anglo Brewery, Commercial Rd

reproduced in The Anglo by Fred Davis, the brewery was erected by Messrs Morrice, Cox and Clarke of London in 1864. It would appear from the start to have been designed to brew pale ales for export to the then British Empire.

In 1871 it was bought by already established brewers Hill, Garton and Company who already owned a large brewery in Southampton. By 1890 Mr Barnard suggests that they owned 16 breweries. However some of the Garton family made Shepton Mallet their home and became very prominent residents. The last of the local Gartons, Colonel Archie Garton is still well remembered though he died in the 1960s. He was an expert on local dialect and encouraged the production of ornate ironwork. Amongst the houses the Gartons lived in are some of the finest in the neighbourhood. Langhorne House, now St Paul's School, Bowlish House and latterly Pylle Manor about three miles south of the town.

41a) The brewery in its prime, circa 1900

One major service the Brewery provided the town from the 1860s until it's closure in 1921

41b) The Anglo Bavarian Brewery circa 1880

41c) Massive outbuildings at Anglo

was the use of the Brewery fire brigade which acted as the only fire brigade for the town and the surrounding area. The Gartons took a very personal interest in this fire brigade which was equipped to a high standard. The occasion of Queen Victoria's Diamond Jubilee in 1897 was celebrated by the gift of an escape ladder by James Garton to the town.

It is reputed that the brewery was the first in Britain to brew lager. There doesn't appear to be any specific use of the word but it is described as specialising in 'Pale' ales and given the 'Bavarian' connection in its name it would seem to have been more than likely that this was the case. The 'Bavarian' element of the name was dropped during the First World War. However the 'German' taint would appear to have stuck and combined with a social trend towards falling beer consumption, and perhaps a focus on other breweries by the Gartons, it shut in 1921.

The massive brewery was then taken over by the Bennett Family and began to be used for more diverse purposes - including the Anglo Cider Company and a revamped Anglo Brewery in the 1930s. Many of the metal Anglo signs and advertising materials would seem to date from this phase. From the start of World War II the site was taken over by the Air Ministry, mainly for storage and distribution purposes and at least part of the site remained in their hands until 1961.

Still under the ownership of the Bennetts the postwar period continued to see the diversification of use on the site. Ownership was then taken on by a local businessman, the late John Haskins, who used part of the site for furniture storage in support of his large retail operation while he continued to develop its use as an industrial estate. It is now home to a number of companies including Brothers Drinks who will be mentioned in the next section.

Later usage of the brewery has done little to alter the fabric and to industrial archeologists, it is a real gem, an almost intact, little altered example of a large 19th century industrial brewery. From the outside it merely appears massive. Exploration inside reveals it to be even larger than it appears. Even the sheds along the northern side, which appear so insignificant alongside the main body of the building, are massive three story high warehouses. The high frontage with the chimney rising behind it are thought to now have some structural problems. It is to be hoped that a solution can be found to these probems. Shepton could ill afford to lose such a marvellous building. The town's swimming pool in is another legacy of the brewery, being constructed in one of the former cooling tanks.

Down in Bowlish exploration of the scrub to the left of the Wells road just past the last yard will reveal a ramshackle shed. Inside can be found the remains of the pumping engine that pumped water up to the brewery - a major source of contention with local landowners. The engine has been stripped of most of its workings and any metal of value, however it still represents an interesting relic. The source of the water was a spring on the opposite side of the valley and the vaulted spring chamber is still below the small 'Spring Cottage' in Back Lane, Darshill.

42) The Anglo pumping engine, Bowlish

Cider, Perry and Alcopops

Farmhouse cider has been a feature of Somerset for many centuries, although it was slow to move into the towns on an industrial scale. It was only during the last quarter of the 19th century that recognized cider firms started to grow and it was well into thw 20th century that Shepton Mallet began to assume a role which now sees it as containing one of the two biggest cider factories in the world.

43) Entrance to former Kilver Street Brewery

The story begins with a small brewery in Kilver Street, behind the former Ship Inn. Although Kilver Street has largely been demolished in the massive post war factory developments and road widening, the archway through to the former brewery can still be seen in the middle of a very interesting but sadly redundant group of buildings still clinging on to the edge of the main A37. It was here that the Showering family had a brewery of a much smaller scale than the other competitors in the town but with a thriving trade delivering beer and cider to pubs around the neighbourhood and to their own pubs in town. In a 1930 directory A. Showering is shown as being the landlord of both the

43a) Kilver St, former Ship Inn and Brewery entrance

Ship Inn and 'Parker's Vaults' (now The Wine Vaults) on the High Street. The family later took over the King's Arms in Leg Square and other pubs in the town.

By the 1930's the Showering family had no fewer than four sons come into the business and through the economic depression managed to start to grow. They experimented with new products such as mineral waters and improved their ciders and other juices. By 1938 they were big enough to purchase the former Jardine's factory site, although this was then used by the National Deposit Friendly Society during the Second World War.

Towards the end of the war people were looking to the future and the likely scarcity of machines and parts was seen to be a coming problem. By 1944 Showerings were campaigning to the ministry to be allowed a new press to replace their old worn out one and, in their support, saying it was essential for local jobs. The ambition

43b) 'Babycham' Kilver Street

of the company was typified by the youngest of the four brothers, Francis, who was experimenting with producing a bottled cider drink which would have wide commercial appeal. Rather surprisingly he found it with a Perry (Pear cider) drink which eventually became the marketing legend 'Babycham' a drink which had a strong appeal to the sweeter palate and caused a social revolution by becoming acceptable for 'respectable'

43c) Gaymer's Cider Factory, Kilver St

43d) A reminder of the past, Kilver Street

women to drink in pubs and clubs, helping to remove previous social stigmas.

It was the success of Babycham which resulted in the huge factory development around the Kilver Street area of town which at one time seemed likely to swamp the whole of Garston Street. The company grew and through the take-over of traditional West Country cider producers such as Coates and Whiteways and more recently Taunton Cider, became the second largest player in the cider market behind Bulmers of Hereford. Along the way the company was taken over by Allied Domeque, Matthew Clark and now a Canadian company Constellation. However, it has recently been given back a cider identity by being given the name Gaymer's Cider. It is rather ironic that this name derives from the one major non West Country acquisition, W. Gaymer's originating in Thetford in Norfolk, a very small cider area compared to Somerset.

Now with prominent popular brands such as Blackthorn, Old English, Autumn Gold, Special Vat, K and Addlestones the company are seeking to develop new top-end of the market ciders.

When the head office moved to Whitchurch in Bristol the luxurious offices developed by the Showering's in the former Jardine's fac-

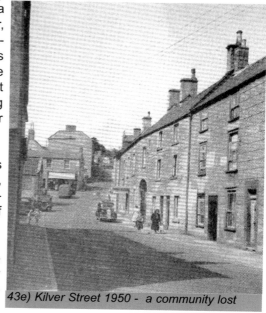

43e) Kilver Street 1950 - a community lost

tory were sold off to the Mulberry Fashion business which has made them their head office, maintaining for fashion shoots and hospitality the marvelous Showering Gardens, now called the Mulberry Gardens.

During the middle part of the 20th century Showerings was not the only cider factory in the town. Anglo Ciders was set up and run by the Bennett's, first of all in the massive remnants of the Anglo Brewery, and then when they were moved from there by the Air Ministry at the start of the war, they carried on down in a former mill down in Darshill. Photographs showing the inside of the factory reveal it to have been much more akin to the traditional farmhouse cider business than a modern factory.

44) Cider making, Anglo Cider Mills, Darshill

The same cannot be said of Brothers Drinks, founded in the 1990s by grandsons of the Showering Brothers - nephews of Francs Showering. They set up a company in buildings to the rear of the former Anglo Brewery to produce a new bottled Perry 'Straight 8'. This marvellous drink, with a powerful 8% alcohol, has never really taken off except perhaps at the Glastonbury Festival. However the company moved into the production and bot-

44a) Inside the Darshill Mill

tling of the then very fashionable 'Alcopops', highly alcoholic fizzy drinks for people whose taste for other alcoholic drinks not developed. Mainly bottling brands for other companies they have become a significant local employer and in the 2001 built an attractive new factory on part of the brewery land. It is a most successful industrial building which has managed to blend in with what was there before without overshadowing the adjoining residential areas.

So the first decade of the 21st century sees Shepton Mallet with two major drinks factories, continuing a tradition of over 150 years.

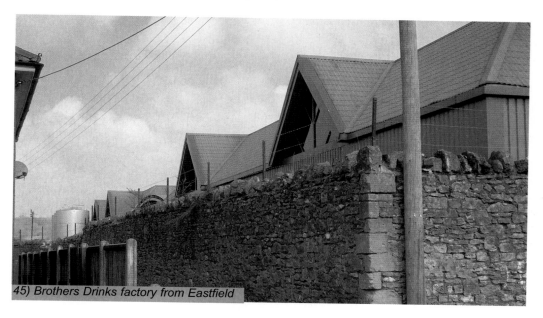

45) Brothers Drinks factory from Eastfield

Parkland

One of the major characteristics of Shepton Mallet that the town must look to conserve over future generations is its rural aspect. Green hills roll down into the town from the top

46) *The Show Field, Cannard's Grave Road*

of the Mendip Hills to the north. Here the typical steep south scarp slope of Mendip loses some of its severity, becoming instead a series of shorter hills. This is probably one of the main reasons for Shepton's position as a communications centre both for road and then rail. From both the eastern and western approaches to the town, fields and woodland cling to the sides of the steep valleys well into the town environs.

Perhaps the best example of the rural approach to the town is from the south. From Cannard's Grave the road into the town centre until recently was open fields on both sides. Now there are modern estates on the eastern side, but to the west it is still largely open fields to within a hundred yards of the town centre. The odd attractive stone barn, individual trees, a row of tall pines and, on occasion, sheep grazing in the Show field, where the Mid-Somerset "Shepton' Show is held every

46a) *'Shepton Show'*

47) *Field Villas, Cannard's Grave Road*

August, give an almost parkland feel. In fact this is close to reality. It is a landscape that was consciously developed and conserved by Sir Frederick Berryman of Field House in the first half of the twentieth century. He was using his brewery wealth to create the illusion of a 'country estate'. It is important that this green tongue is conserved to protect the rural aspect of the town. The new Park Medical Practice built in a robust and solid neo-rural style echoing the mullioned facade of old farm house, should be the last new building allowed on this stretch. Opposite the Show Field is Field View, an interesting row of

48) *Park Medical Practice, Cannard's Grave Road*

late Victorian buildings presumably built by some property speculator for the 'civil service' class of Shepton. They still make one of the more interesting groupings in the town

27b) Parkland at Langhorne House

and retain their attractive outlook across the fields.

Even within the town there is a strong tradition of park land which, although originally owned by the wealthy, has always been places where major events of the town have taken part. Fortunately, two of our urban parks have been conserved within the grounds of two of the schools.

Langhorne Park is now the grounds of St Paul's School. The house was built in the mid-19th century but quickly established a park. Traces of the pattern of formal gardens can

49) Whitstone House, Town Street

26b) Parkland at Whitstone

still be found in the lawns to the south of the school. There is still the copse - an attractive distance from the house - though rather inhibiting to the inclusion of more football pitches in the field. The southern end of the field is now taken over by the Roman Catholic Church.

The owners of this park in the second half of the 19th century allowed it to be used for some significant town events. Newspaper reports from the 1860s tell of some huge horticultural shows which sound as if the entire population of the town took part. It was here in the 1870s that the Evercreech Farmers Ploughing match metamorphosed into the Mid-Somerset Show and for about 20 years, continued to be held here.

The second school set in parkland is Whitstone. Whitstone House is a remarkable interesting old house down in Town Lane. It appears to have a large 18th century frontage. However, even a quick glance suggests that the bulk of the building is older, and was possibly even bigger. The main part of the park was sold to the County Council in the 1930's and land next to the house itself has become a small modern development of bungalows.

This park too was often made available for public events in the town, the Mid-Somerset Show was held here in the 1890s before it moved to its home of the last 100 years at Field. The little used western side of the school grounds still conserve many of the park features. Specimen trees are slowly reaching their sell-by date. The attractive little stream, a tributary running down the valley to join the Sheppey is now probably considered more of a health and safety issue, and the hedges outline what was probably once a 'secret' garden area with an attractive aspect of the church over the roofs of the prison.

Collett Park is just about unique in the area. No other Mendip Town has such a glorious public park in the centre of town. Many people have referred to it as the jewel of Shepton

50) Children enjoying Collett Park

Mallet. It has been added to over the years and now can be said to include the disused railway line and the attractive wildlife pond on the other side in the new extension on the edge of the Tadley Acres development.

The park is now just coming up to its Centenary, being rather surprisingly totally 20th century. It was a gift to the town by a local boy made good. John Kyte Collett was born in the town in about 1836. He can be found on the census of 1841 as John Collett, 5, living in Garston Street with his mother Julia (by that time a widow), who was listed as a Grocer, and his sister Anne who was 3. Locally educated he was apprenticed to a draper in Bristol and then set up his own business in South Wales. In 1900 he bought some of the fields in a sale of the Langhorne Estate and set about constructing a park for the town. The legend is that as a young boy he had been chucked out of Langhorne Park when playing there and had decided to provide a park for the people of the town.

50a) The Bandstand

The Park was first opened in 1906 and although it has sometimes been a worry to the local authorities as to who is to bear the cost of maintenance, it has been a source of pride ever since. Every year on the first Saturday of June, weather permitting, the Collett Day festival is held. Unlike

50b) The ornamental pond, Collett Park

many 'fairs' this has remained a strictly 'town' event. Local charities with their stalls seeking to raise funds from around 3,000 townspeople who each year bring their children for a wander around, coming away with bedding plants, second-hand book, and a vast collection of raffle tickets for local causes.

The park has also seen history. In the Second World War troops returning from Dunkirk were unloaded from trains at the nearby station and left to rest in the park. Later in the

50c) Early Days in Collett Park

war the eastern end of the park was used as a temporary army camp. The great winds of 1989 brought down some trees which were quickly replanted. In the past the Town Band played in the gracious bandstand on Sunday afternoons in the summer and, in the days before many had motor cars to whisk them out of town, the local population would turn out to relax and enjoy themselves.

Vandalism has always been a problem. Today school head teachers have to give periodic lectures to their pupils. During World War II a long-suffering park keeper appeared in the magistrates court charged with dunking a youngster head first in the pond. Although guilty the punishment was minimal and it was clear where the magistrat's sympathies lay.

Mention must also be made of town historian Fred Davis MBE who was park keeper through the 1980s and 90s until his retirement in 2002. With the help of his brother Roy and a small band of volunteers and work experience youngsters he continued to maintain the green swards of the park on a small budget from the town council. His office in the yard to the south of the park became a magnet for visitors trying to find out about the history of the town and their families.

In these modern times such a large park in such a small town may be considered an anachronism. However, whatever time of day you go in there it is being used - People walking their dogs, clutching their little plastic bags to proudly pick up the feces; mothers with young children, push chairs parked inside the play areas, or looking at the birds in the aviaries; school children sprawled on the grass after school, or during the holidays, idly kicking a football around. Collett Park is still very much a part of the ongoing traditions of Shepton Mallet.

50d) Tranquil scene, Collett Park

Bibliography

Even in such a short study as this it is amazing how many sources are at least looked at. The following is a list of those I have consciously supplemented my knowledge with during the writing of this work.

Shepton Mallet	John Farbrother 1859
The Shepton Mallet Story	Fred Davis MBE 1969
A Shepton Mallet Camera	Fred Davis MBE 1984
A Shepton Mallet Camera (Vol 2)	Fred Davis MBE 1986
A Shepton Mallet Camera (Vol 3)	Fred Davis MBE 1992
The Anglo	Fred Davis MBE 1995
A Shepton Mallet Camera (Vol 4)	Fred Davis MBE 1996
Shepton Mallet Prison	Francis Disney BEM 1998
Shepton Show	Alan Stone 2002
A Town Alive (SM in World War II)	Alan Stone and others 2004
A Journey Through Time (SM Parish Church)	Joyce & Alan Hodgson 2001
Ashwick. Coal, Ale and Pasture	Ed Penny Stokes 2002
Pigot & Co's Directory 1830	Facsimile Edition 1993
A History of a Mendip Town	David Rossington (Unpublished)
Shepton Mallet Baptist Church	Bill Krouwel 2001
Norah Fry Hospital -Design Brief	Carlisle Jessop Architects 2003
An Archaeological Assessment of SM	Clare Gathercole 2003

Reference has also been made to various editions of the Shepton Mallet Journal. I have to thank my wife Christine who has transcribed the 1841 cencus.

Apologies to any sources I may have missed.

Photo Index to Map and Text

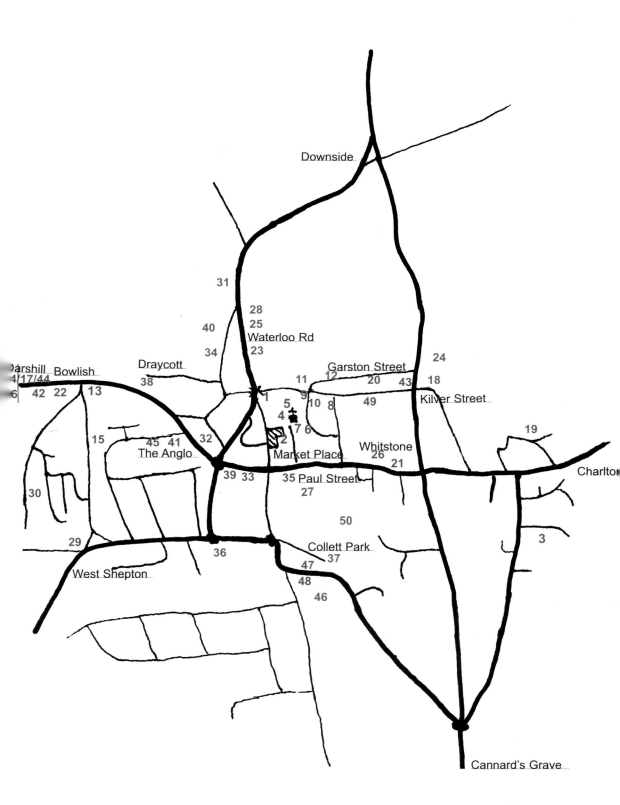

Downside

31

28
25
Waterloo Rd
40
34   23

Draycott   Garston Street   24
arshill   Bowlish   12   20   43   18
4/17/44   38   11   Kilver Street
6   42   22   13   1   9
5   10 8   49
4   7 6
15   45 41   32   2   Whitstone
The Anglo   Market Place   26
30   39 33   35 Paul Street 21   19
27
50
29
36   Collett Park 37   3
West Shepton   47
48
46

Cannard's Grave